This book belongs to:

_____

My name is Lionel Messi, and I'm a football player.
If you live in the USA, you may think of touchdowns and
tackling, but here in Argentina, football is the same as socce

I play as a forward, which means I'm close to the other team's goal

In other words,
it's all on me to score the goal and win the game.
Have you ever had to help your team to win?
It's not easy! How did I wind up here? Well...

I was born in 1987. My parents were hard workers, and loved soccer. I practiced playing soccer with my brothers, and we were unstoppable.

While other children were in preschool, my dad was coaching me.
Everyone helped me out on my dream. Even my grandmother, who I still look up to today.

When I was six, I joined a kids' soccer team.
I wanted to make our games just as exciting as
an adult's so I was ready to put on a show.

They had fun as I played many tricks with the ball, and by the time I was 12, I scored around 500 goals!

But there was a problem. I watched my friends and teammates grow from children to young adults, but I stayed the same size.

As it turns out, I couldn't grow any more.
I was too old to play against children my height,
and too small to play against children my age.

My father wanted to get me medicine to make me grow but it was too expensive. It would take a while.

So I did what I knew I should do. I kept playing.

I ran along the field. My short legs took me far.

With my tiny feet, I kicked the ball right into the goal.

When I was 14, I finally got the medicine I needed, and I soon grew like the other kids.
I joined Barcelona's youth academy, and I played all sorts of games.

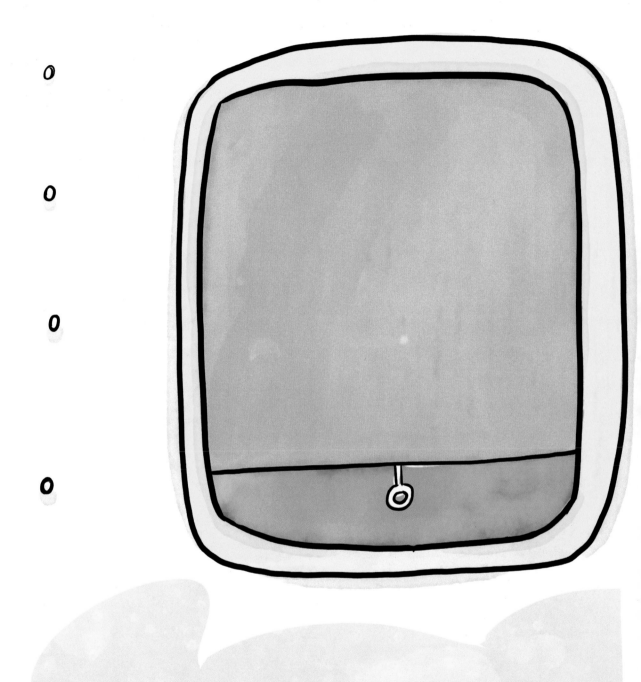

My first season, I was on top!

I scored many goals for my team, and

we rose to be the best players of the season.

It wasn't always easy. One time, I fell and broke my cheekbone.

I could still play, but I had this protector over my cheek so I wouldn't hurt it again.

I tried playing with it, but it was slowing me down.
My teammates needed me! What should I do?

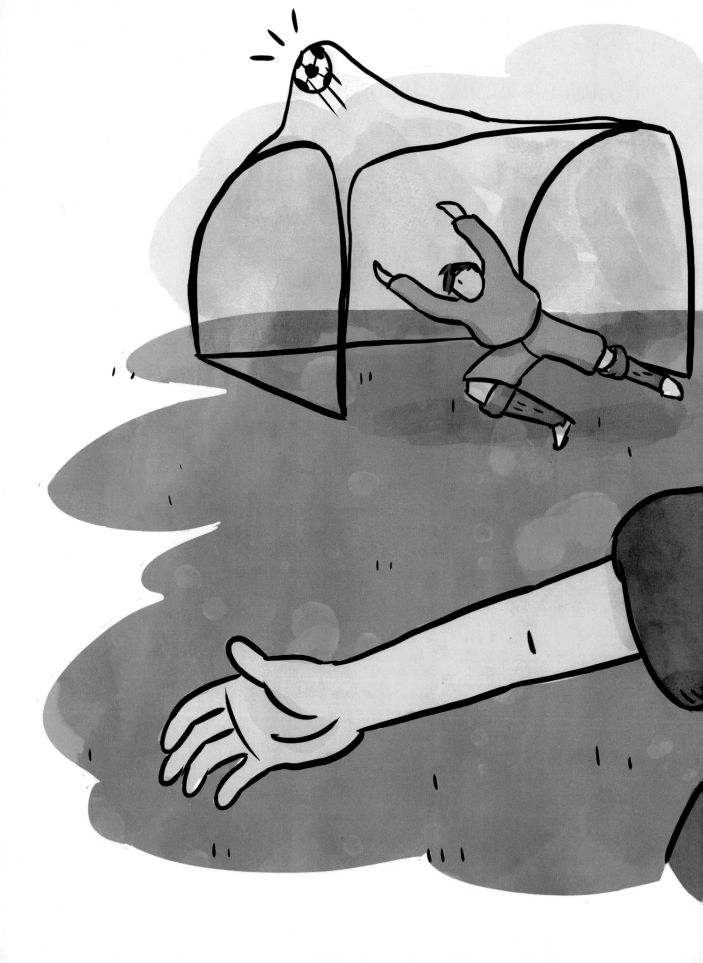

I decided to take it off. I threw away that thing and won the game! I took a risk, and that propelled me even higher.

Since then, I've done nothing but play soccer..
I play for Barcelona at the club level,
and I also play for my national country Argentina.

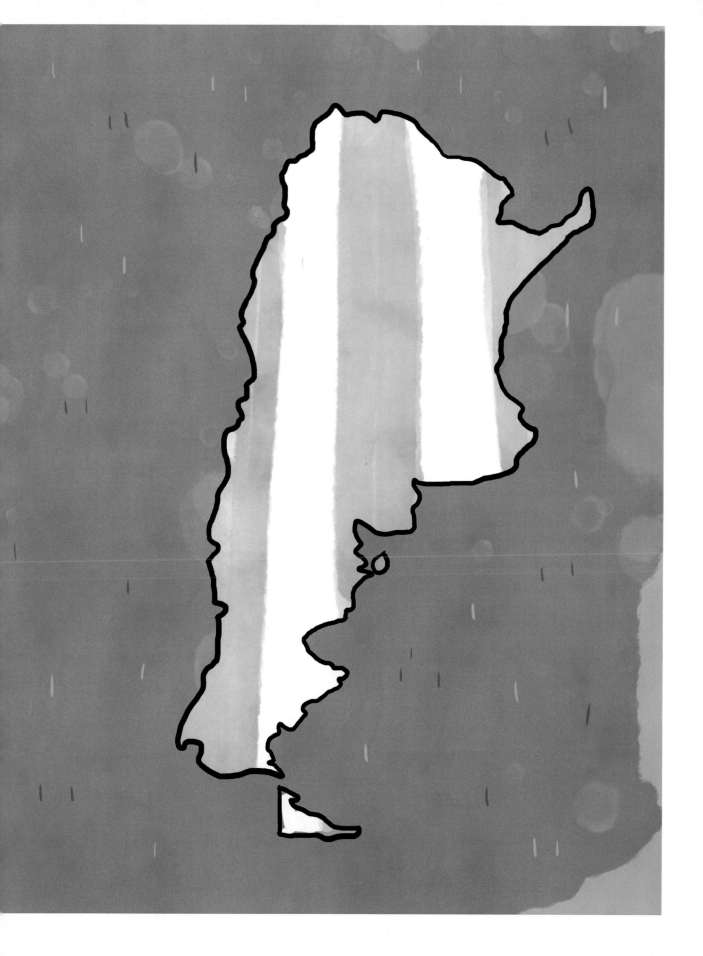

People say that I am the best soccer player of all time. I've broken records, lead my team to victory, and passed anything the world has thrown at me.

But it wasn't all because of me.

My family helped me, and all my friends did too.

To win, you need to surround yourself with good people.

Read more about my life story here...

LIONEL MESSI
THE RISE TO STARDOM
Roy Brandon

Made in the USA
Monee, IL
14 September 2022

13948900R00024